W9-BLN-033

What's for lunch?

Peas

© 1999 by Franklin Watts
96 Leonard Street
London
EC2A 4XD

First American edition 1999 by Franklin Watts/Children's Press
A Division of Grolier Publishing
90 Sherman Turnpike
Danbury, CT 06816

Editor: Samantha Armstrong
Series Designer: Kirstie Billingham
Designer: Jason Anscomb
Consultant: Processors and Growers Research Organisation
Reading Consultant: Prue Goodwin, Reading and Language Information
Centre, Reading.

ISBN 0-516-21549-3

A catalog record for this book is available from the Library of Congress

Visit Franklin Watts/Children's Press on the Internet at:
http://publishing.grolier.com

Printed in Hong Kong

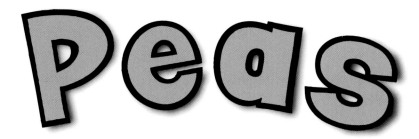

What's for lunch?

Peas

Claire Llewellyn

CHILDREN'S PRESS®

A Division of Grolier Publishing

NEW YORK • LONDON • HONG KONG • SYDNEY
DANBURY, CONNECTICUT

Today we are having peas for lunch.
Peas are vegetables.
They contain **vitamins, minerals, fiber,** and **protein.**
They help us grow and stay healthy.

Peas are the seeds of the pea plant.
They grow inside cases called **pods.**
Most kinds of peas are taken out of their
pods, or shelled, before we eat them.
But we don't shell **snow** peas and **sugarsnap**
peas—we eat the pod with the peas inside.

sugarsnap
peas

Peas are grown all over the world.
In spring, farmers plant the seeds
in rows. This is called **drilling.**
The seeds are peas from
last year's **crop.**

In the soil the seeds split open and grow a **root** called a **radicle**. Then they sprout **shoots** that grow up through the soil. The young **seedlings** produce green leaves and side shoots, and grow into plants.

The farmers care for the growing crop. They spray it with **fungicide** and **insecticide** to protect it from diseases and insects.

In early summer, flowers grow on the pea plants. Soon the petals drop off, and the pods begin to form. Inside each pod are up to ten tiny peas that start to swell. A month later, the peas inside the pods are sweet, juicy, and green.

The peas are **harvested** by huge pea **viners.**
The machine takes the peas out of the pods.

Later the empty pods are plowed back into the field as **fertilizer**.

The peas are poured into large containers and taken to nearby factories. Most of the peas we eat are **frozen.** The peas are frozen within three hours of being picked so they are really fresh.

In the freezing factory, the peas are graded, or sorted into different sizes. They are cooked for just one minute, to kill any germs, and then blasted with ice-cold air. This freezes the peas and stops them from sticking together.

frozen peas

The frozen peas are packed into
bags and stored in freezers.
Refrigerated trucks transport them to stores.

Sometimes the peas are soaked in **brine** and
put into cans. This helps them to last longer.

Snow peas are grown in places where it is hot, like parts of Africa. When the peas are ready for harvesting, workers pick them and pack them into bags.

The bags are flown to many countries around the world. The peas are still crisp and fresh by the time they arrive.

snow peas

Some peas are dried and split. They can be used to make split pea soup.

Some peas are not harvested until they are hard. They have to be soaked in water before they are ready to eat.

split peas

Peas are eaten
in different ways around
the world. There are peas
in risotto, an Italian dish.

They are in pakora,
an Indian snack.

Peas are also
added to paella,
a Spanish dish.
Peas are sweet,
tasty, and good
for you, too.

29

Glossary

brine	salty water that stops food decaying and helps it to last
crop	what farmers grow in their fields
drill	to plant seeds in rows
fertilizer	something that helps plants grow
fiber	something that helps us digest our food
frozen	when something is so cold it is hard and stays fresh
fungicide	something that kills plant disease
harvest	to take the crop from the fields
insecticide	something that kills insects
minerals	materials found in rocks and also in our food. Minerals help us stay healthy
pods	the cases in which peas grow

protein	something found in food such as peas which helps build and repair the body
radicle	the first root from the pea seed
root	the part of a plant that grows underground and takes moisture and goodness from the soil
seedlings	very young plants that grow from a seed
shoots	the new parts of a plant that grow above the soil
shell	to take the peas out of their pods
snow pea	a kind of pea that is eaten in its pod
sugarsnap pea	a kind of pea that is eaten in its pod
viners	machines that pick pea plants and remove the peas from the pods
vitamins	something found in vegetables and fruit that keeps us healthy

Index

Picture credits: 7 Chris Fairclough, © Franklin Watts; 8, 9, 10 Holt Studios International / Nigel Cattlin; 11 Courtesy of Birds Eye Wall's Ltd; 12-13, 15 Holt Studios International / Nigel Cattlin; 16-17 Courtesy of FMC Harvesters; 19 Holt Studios International / Willem Harinck; 21, 23 Courtesy of Birds Eye Wall's Ltd; 24 Panos Pictures / Ron Giling. Cover Steve Sho All other photographs Tim Ridley, Wells Street Studios, London.
With thanks to Aiden Senior and Alex Wright.